CATS SET IV

AMERICAN SHORTHAIR CATS

Nancy Furstinger
ABDO Publishing Company

visit us at
www.abdopub.com

Published by ABDO Publishing Company, 4940 Viking Drive, Edina, Minnesota 55435.
Copyright © 2006 by Abdo Consulting Group, Inc. International copyrights reserved in
all countries. No part of this book may be reproduced in any form without written
permission from the publisher. The Checkerboard Library™ is a trademark and logo of
ABDO Publishing Company.

Printed in the United States.

Cover Photo: Ron Kimball
Interior Photos: Animals Animals pp. 9, 15, 19; Corbis pp. 4, 5, 7, 11, 12, 17, 18;
    Ron Kimball pp. 13, 21

Series Coordinator: Megan Murphy
Editors: Stephanie Hedlund, Megan Murphy
Art Direction: Neil Klinepier

Library of Congress Cataloging-in-Publication Data

Furstinger, Nancy.
    American shorthair cats / Nancy Furstinger.
        p. cm. -- (Cats. Set IV)
    ISBN 1-59679-264-7
        1. American shorthair cat.--Juvenile literature. I. Title.

SF449.A45F87 2005
636.8'22--dc22
                                                    2005042127

CONTENTS

LIONS, TIGERS, AND CATS

More than 3,500 years ago, people in Egypt began taming wildcats. These cats hunted rats and mice that swarmed into granaries where the harvests were stored. The Egyptians thought cats brought prosperity and good fortune.

Egyptians often painted cats on the walls of their tombs.

Domestic cats can trace their ancestry back to these African wildcats. Today, there are more than 40 different **breeds** of domestic cats. They all belong to the **Felidae** family, which contains 38 different species.

Domestic cats are related to lions, tigers, leopards, cheetahs, and pumas. All share similar **traits**. They communicate by meowing or roaring. They use sharp teeth and claws for hunting. And, they enjoy catnapping!

Many similarities can be seen between this African wildcat and the domestic cats in homes today.

AMERICAN SHORTHAIR CATS

The first cats arrived in North America with the first European settlers. Records show that several cats sailed aboard the *Mayflower* with the Pilgrims in 1620. These cats hunted mice and rats on ships, and later on farms in America.

The cats soon adapted to the New World. They grew larger than their European cousins. America's first working cats eventually became a popular **breed**. The American shorthair developed from these cats.

The **Cat Fanciers' Association** recognized American shorthairs as a breed in 1906. They were first registered as the shorthair and later as the **domestic** shorthair. The **breed** name was officially changed to American shorthair in 1966.

At the Second Annual Cat Show, a brown tabby American shorthair like this one was offered for sale for $2,500. This was a fortune in 1896.

QUALITIES

The American shorthair is considered the native cat of America. Overall, it is a healthy **breed**. Since the arrival of the original shorthairs from Europe, this cat has adapted well and remains robust.

Centuries later, American shorthairs continue to catch mice. They have a strong hunting instinct. These cats are also good-natured and playful. They are friendly with children, other cats, and dogs.

American shorthairs are very smart. They have been known to open closet or cupboard doors. They often greet their family at the door after waiting in the window for their return. They can even be trained to stay off the dinner table!

American shorthair cats are often used in television commercials because they can be trained easily. These kittens love having their picture taken, too!

COAT AND COLOR

The American shorthair has a coat for all seasons. After arriving in North America, its fur grew thick to protect it from damp and cold weather.

Their coats come in a variety of colors and designs. More than 80 different colors and patterns are possible. They can be solid, shaded, smoke, or **tabby** patterned. The silver tabby is the most familiar.

The American shorthair's eye color depends on its coat color. Most shorthairs have gold eyes. However, silver cats usually have green eyes. White cats may be blue-eyed or odd-eyed. Odd-eyed is when one eye is blue and one eye is gold.

The classic tabby pattern consists of black markings decorating the coat. The pattern can form buttons, butterfly wings, necklaces, and bracelets. A large black M marks the forehead of this tabby.

SIZE

The American shorthair is a medium to large cat with a muscular body. Males range from 11 to 15 pounds (5 to 7 kg). Females are smaller and range from 8 to 12 pounds (4 to 5 kg).

American shorthairs are athletic cats. They have deep, broad chests and well-developed shoulders. Their legs are strong and built for hunting. Their medium-length tail tapers toward a rounded tip.

American shorthair males often develop jowls. A jowl is loose skin around the cheeks, lower jaw, and throat.

These powerful cats are built to stalk and catch prey.

American shorthairs have broad, round heads with square noses. Their large, wide eyes are round at the bottom and almond shaped at the top. And, they have wide-set ears that are rounded at the tips.

CARE

Cats use their rough tongues as combs to clean their fur. But, American shorthairs should also be groomed with a brush or comb to remove loose hair. This helps prevent hair balls from forming in their stomachs.

Cats are generally neat animals. A natural instinct for them is to bury their waste. Train your American shorthair to use a **litter box**. Keep it in a quiet place away from food and water. And, be sure to remove waste from the box daily.

Toys such as a ball or a catnip mouse will bring out your cat's playful nature. However, it will enjoy a piece of crumpled paper or a paper bag just as much. A scratching post will keep your cat from destroying the furniture and carpet.

Your American shorthair will need to visit the veterinarian for a yearly checkup and **vaccines**. The veterinarian can also **spay** or **neuter** your pet during this visit.

While friendly and affectionate, the American shorthair needs its space, too. It will also need a scratching post if it is not allowed outside.

FEEDING

Cats are meat eaters. Even **domestic** cats need meat in their diets. Feed your American shorthair food that contains protein, such as beef, poultry, or fish. Commercial cat food is recommended because it contains all the **nutrients** your cat needs.

There are three kinds of commercial cat food. They are dry, semimoist, and canned. Each kind offers different recipes based on age, weight, and health. The food label will tell you how much and how often to feed your pet.

Always have clean, fresh water available for your cat. Many kittens love to drink milk. But, milk is not a natural part of a cat's diet. So, it should be considered a treat. Too much milk can cause stomach problems, especially in older cats.

*Opposite page: **With any breed of cat, serve their food in a stainless steel, plastic, or ceramic bowl at the same time every day.***

KITTENS

These tabby kittens are still wobbly on their feet when they try to move around.

American shorthair mothers pass along their sweet natures to their kittens. Cats are **pregnant** for 63 to 65 days. They give birth to about four kittens in each **litter**.

Kittens are born blind and deaf. They drink their mother's milk. When they are three to five weeks old, kittens can start eating soft food. By eight weeks old, the majority of their food should be solid.

American shorthair kittens begin to play and explore within their first three weeks. By then they can see and hear, and their teeth start coming in. When kittens are 9 to 12 weeks old, they can go home with new families.

Kittens depend on their mother for nearly everything until they are about nine weeks old.

BUYING A KITTEN

American shorthairs can live for 15 to 20 years. They become attached to their human companions. So before adopting a kitten, make sure everyone in the family is devoted to caring for it.

The American shorthair is one of the ten most popular **breeds** of cats. You can buy a **purebred** kitten from a breeder. Rescue shelters, veterinary clinics, and pet shows may also have cats for adoption.

Look for a kitten that is active and alert. A curious, playful kitten might come over to inspect you. If the kitten has gleaming fur, bright eyes, and clean ears and nose, it is healthy. This could be the perfect pet for your family!

Opposite page: *These adorable American shorthair kittens would love to come home with you!*

GLOSSARY

breed - a group of animals sharing the same appearance and characteristics. A breeder is a person who raises animals. Raising animals is often called breeding them.

Cat Fanciers' Association (CFA) - a group that sets the standards for judging all breeds of cats.

domestic - animals that are tame.

Felidae - the scientific Latin name for the cat family.

litter - all of the kittens born at one time to a mother cat.

litter box - a box filled with cat litter, which is similar to sand. Cats use litter boxes to dispose of their waste.

neuter (NOO-tuhr) - to remove a male animal's reproductive organs.

nutrient - a substance found in food and used in the body to promote growth, maintenance, and repair.

pregnant - having one or more babies growing within the body.

purebred - an animal whose parents are both from the same breed.

spay - to remove a female animal's reproductive organs.

tabby - the striped or splotchy pattern of a cat's coat. A cat with this pattern is often called a tabby cat.

trait - a quality that distinguishes one person or group from another.

vaccine (vak-SEEN) - a shot given to animals or humans to prevent them from getting an illness or disease.

WEB SITES

To learn more about American shorthair cats, visit ABDO Publishing Company on the World Wide Web at **www.abdopub.com**. Web sites about these cats are featured on our Book Links page. These links are routinely monitored and updated to provide the most current information available.

INDEX